For Mom, with thoughts of fun trips
out in our younger years. JG

To Ann — just because. KR

Text copyright © 2018 by James Gladstone
Illustrations copyright © 2018 by Karen Reczuch
Published in Canada and the USA in 2018 by Groundwood Books

Groundwood Books / House of Anansi Press
groundwoodbooks.com

We acknowledge for their financial support of our publishing
program the Canada Council for the Arts, the Ontario Arts
Council and the Government of Canada.

Canada Council   **Conseil des Arts**
for the Arts   **du Canada**

ONTARIO ARTS COUNCIL
CONSEIL DES ARTS DE L'ONTARIO
an Ontario government agency
un organisme du gouvernement de l'Ontario

With the participation of the Government of Canada | **Canadä**
Avec la participation du gouvernement du Canada

Library and Archives Canada Cataloguing in Publication

Gladstone, James, author
Turtle pond / James Gladstone ; Karen Reczuch, illustrator

Issued in print and electronic formats.
ISBN 978-1-55498-910-2 (hardcover). —
ISBN 978-1-55498-911-9 (PDF)

1. Turtles — Juvenile literature. I. Reczuch, Karen, illustrator
II. Title.

QL666.C5G55 2018   j597.92   C2017-905267-5
C2017-905268-3

The illustrations were made with graphite pencil and watercolor.
Design by Michael Solomon
Printed and bound in Malaysia

FSC
www.fsc.org

MIX
Paper from
responsible sources
FSC® C012700

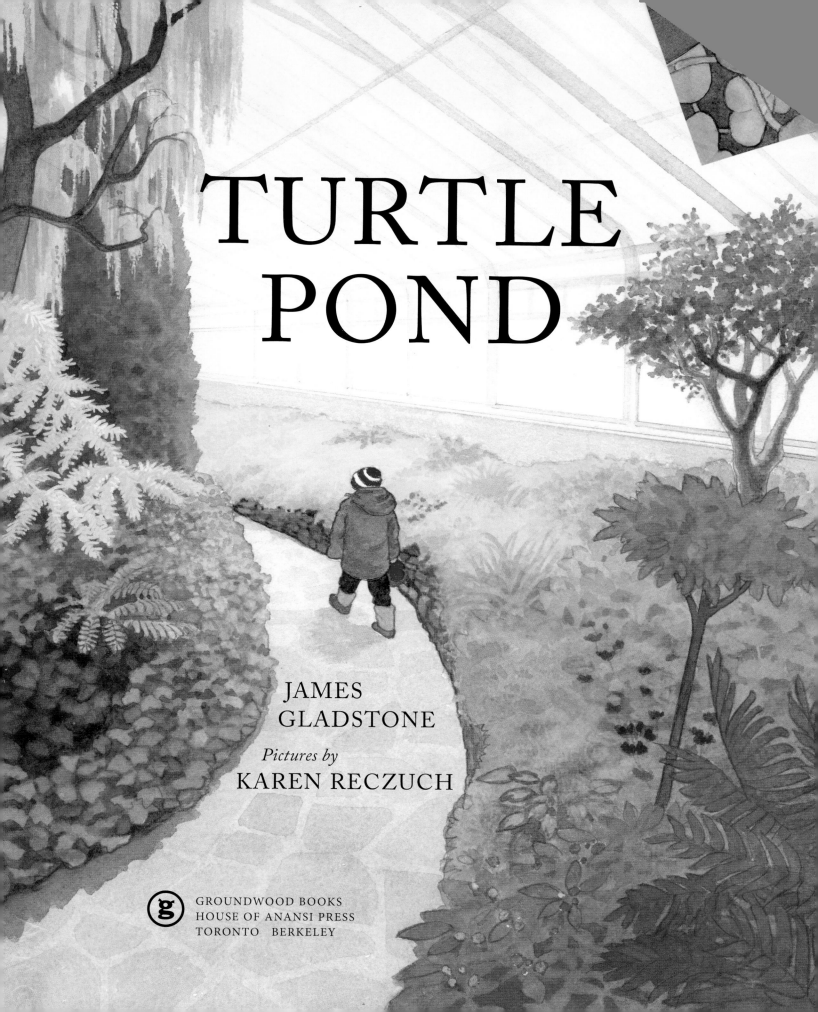

TURTLE
POND

JAMES
GLADSTONE

Pictures by
KAREN RECZUCH

GROUNDWOOD BOOKS
HOUSE OF ANANSI PRESS
TORONTO BERKELEY

Turtles …
in hidden corners
and secret hollows
beneath the wet rocks,
way at the bottom of turtle pond.

Resting
under the water —
they stay so long there.
When do they breathe air?
The sleeping turtles of turtle pond.

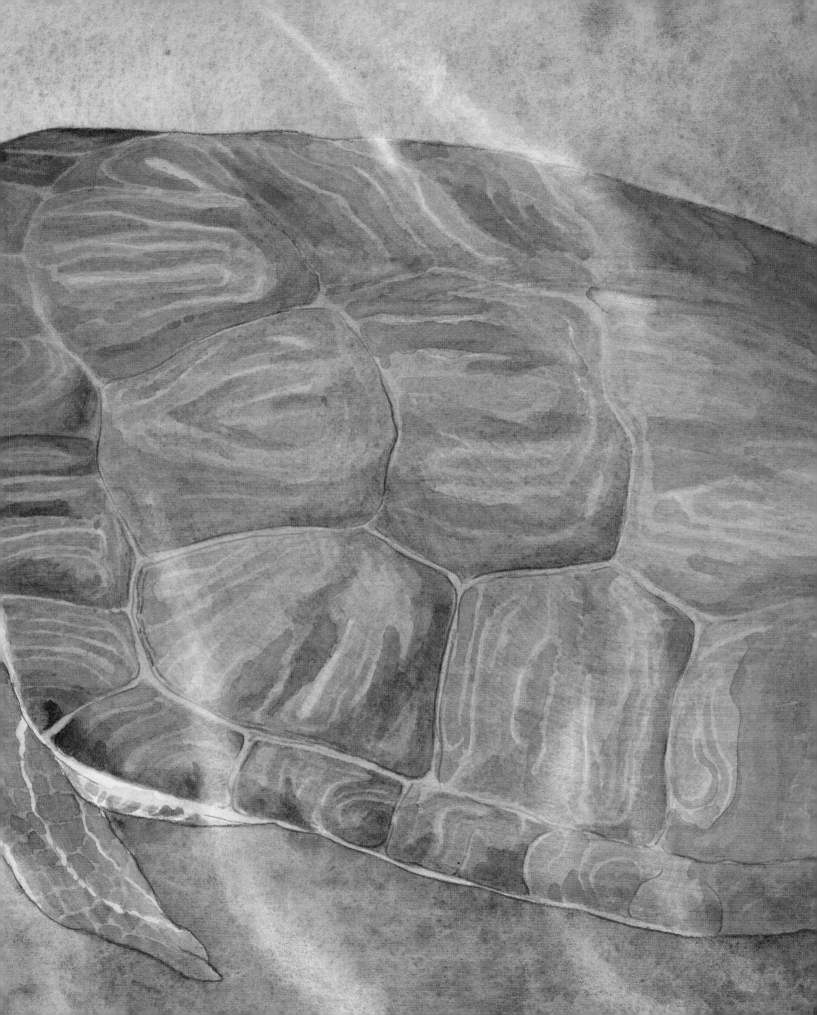

Springtime …
young turtles swimming.
They play together
and chase each other
from top to bottom of turtle pond.

Tummies …
see how they glisten
when wet with water.
Bellies gleaming,
squiggly spots on yellow-green in turtle pond.

Big wheel
turns in a circle,
makes wavy water.
One turtle dives in!
It bobs and bounces in turtle pond.

Wants out
of wavy water!
Slipping and sliding,
clinging to wet rock …
How will it get out of turtle pond?

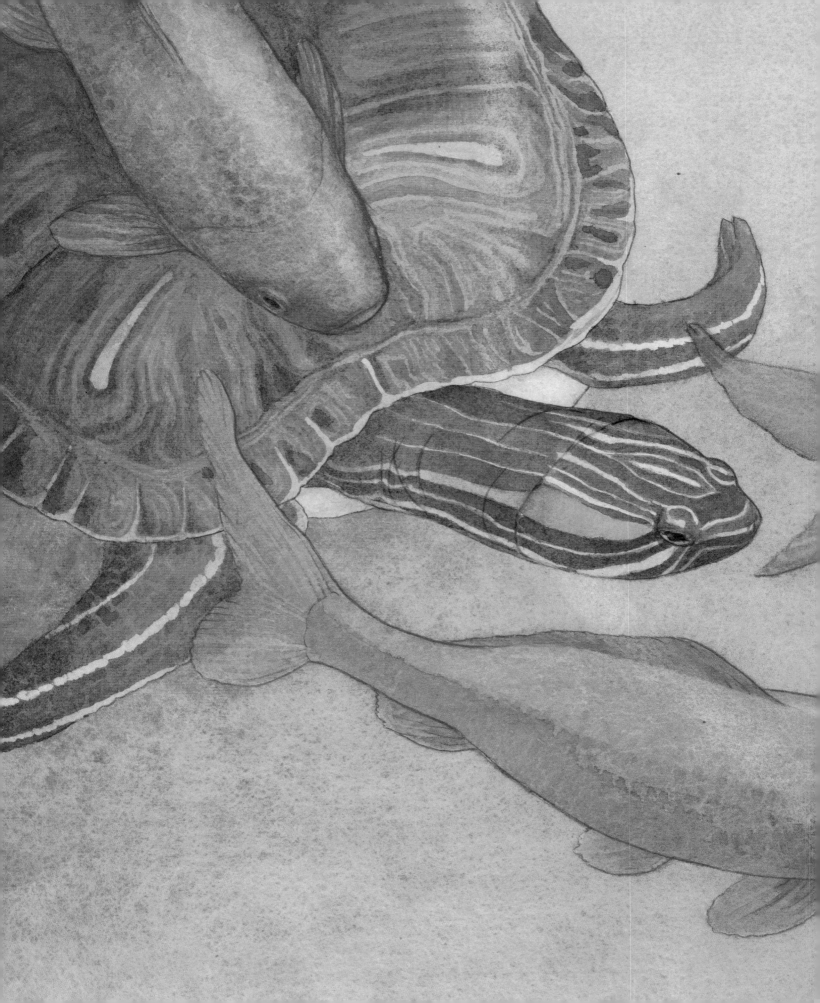

Gliding
under fat goldfish,
it swims up around them
in turtle circles,
poking at tail fins in turtle pond.

Lunchtime …
snaps up a mouthful
of green specks on water.
What is it eating?
It's time for feeding at turtle pond.

Summer …
stretched out in sunlight,
turtles are basking,
warming their bodies
on all the dry rocks of turtle pond.

Slowly,
their mouths are moving.
Are turtles speaking?
We try to hear them,
the sounds they're making at turtle pond.

Piled high —
one, two, three, four, five!
They climb on each other.
Why do they do that?
A stack of turtles at turtle pond.

Green heads
poke out of hard shells.
Can turtles see us
or even hear us?
We watch and wonder at turtle pond.

Runners
race on the footbridge,
too fast for turtles
who pull their heads in,
hiding in hard shells at turtle pond.

Autumn …
when days are shorter
and turtles scatter
to search for sunlight
in nooks and crannies of turtle pond.

Look, there!
One's on the footpath
that people walk on.
Carry it gently
back to the water of turtle pond.

Big one
is always sleeping.
It hangs off dry rocks.
Watch what you're doing!
Plop — into the water of turtle pond.

Nighttime,
when stars are twinkling …
What is it like here?
Are turtles sleeping
or moonlight swimming in turtle pond?

Cold days …
dark winter's coming.
Where are the turtles?
Quietly dozing,
way at the bottom of turtle pond.

AUTHOR'S NOTE

It's hard to say exactly what it is, but there's something about turtles that captivates us. Why else would people, young and old, stop to watch them bask in the sun, climb over rocks or swim idly through the water?

One thing we can say about turtles is that they are ancient. Early species of turtles lived more than two hundred million years ago. Their descendants have adapted to live in environments throughout the world, in deserts, rivers, oceans and forests. About the only places you won't find turtles are in the polar regions.

Today there are close to 320 species of turtles living in the world. Many of those species are threatened with extinction. So it may seem odd that *Turtle Pond* features a species — the Red-eared Slider — that is far from endangered. In fact, the Red-eared Slider is so successful that it is considered an invasive species in many places. To be fair to the Red-ears, they have become invasive in large part due to the vast numbers we have bred as pets.

It is the Red-ears that live in the pond of my local public gardens. Invasive though they may be, they are still turtles. And turtles fascinate and delight me. So maybe the millions of Red-ears can lead to some good after all. Perhaps the pleasure they bring can inspire us to learn about and care for the many threatened species of turtles in the world.

I hope so.